Kingdom

Brian Donohue

Acknowledgements

I hope you enjoy reading this book. The teaching material comes from a series I teach to students on the Kingdom of God. I tried to write as I speak. This book is designed to be read out loud in a small group setting.

If I had to pick two authors who have influenced me the most in my thinking on this subject, I would have to say C.S. Lewis and Dallas Willard. I have read so many books, that I hesitate to say any of the concepts are original to me but I believe most of the stories are mine.

Thank you Nick, Amanda and Lesley for editing the manuscript.

Send me an e-mail at cuirim@aol if you have any thoughts you wish to share after reading the book.

Brian Donohue
Madison Heights, Virginia

Table of Contents

1
The Corner Pole

I have wanted to live on a farm. As a suburban kid growing up in Baltimore, this dream was difficult to realize. My parents let me have some chickens, and for a few years we had Roberto the goat, but a farm, a real farm, that would have to wait. I met my wife Kirsten in Chicago. After we got married, we lived in a one room apartment and my range of agrarian expression was limited to a fish tank.

On Saturdays, I walked into town and bought a fish or two from the pet store. I remember sitting in our entry way in front of the fish tank, watching the fish swim around the plants and rock formations. Sometimes I would sit for hours looking at the little world I had created. After a while, Kirsten usually called down the stairs asking me what I was doing....nothing I suppose....just looking... but it was more than that. I was happy.

A few months later we left Chicago intending to live with my parents in Baltimore for a few months before heading off to work in the Andes Mountains of Venezuela. Plans changed quickly and we ended up at a church in Virginia starting up a youth program. I had never thought I would own a home, but housing prices were so low, it soon became a real possibility. We began to look for a little place where we could have a farm and start our family. After a year of searching, Kirsten came in one day with the newspaper in her hand and said, "I have found the place."

She was right. She had found the place, just two miles from downtown, on the crest of a small hill at the end of a quiet street was a house surrounded by six acres of trash and cars. The grass was three feet high and weeds had grown over the school bus in the back yard. In the middle of this auto junkyard sat a dilapidated house built in the 1800's. We were home and we knew it.

Soon the paperwork was completed and we were living our dream. We spent our spare time reclaiming the place, one trip to the dump at a time. After six months, the land was cleared and we were ready to set up our farm. Money was in short supply and I soon realized that fence poles would be too expensive. For a week or two I was discouraged...how can you have a farm without fences? And how would we ever will we ever come up with the money for 300 fence poles?

I shared my dilemma with my neighbor, Donald. He had the solution. In his woods, stood a grove of tall straight locust trees that I could use for poles. He taught me how to use a chain saw and drop a tree. I learned how to split the poles with a wedge and shave the bark off with an ax. I hauled the poles up the hill one by one, and laid them in the field beside our home. Soon I had enough to get started.

One sunny February morning, I bought a post hole digger and began to build my fence. I went to the corner and dug my first hole, two feet deep, and stuck in my first pole. I was on my way. The ground was as soft as chocolate cake and with the exception of a rock or two, I made steady progress. After sinking my corner pole, I took five steps and put in the second pole. I took five more steps and jammed the post hole digger in what I thought was a good spot for the third pole and then walked back to the corner. At the corner, I looked down the line to see if I had placed the hole correctly.

Usually it took two or three tries before I got it right. I repeated this process over and over again. It was going quicker than I had expected. These were real fence poles and I would soon have a real pasture. I moved down the line, always looking back on my previous holes before setting the next one. I went to bed that night a tired but happy man.

The next morning, I looked down the fence line as I drove by on the way to the office. I expected to feel some degree of satisfaction at seeing my first real farm project, but that is not what I felt. From the road, I could see something I could not see yesterday..... my fence line was crooked, really crooked.

How had I made such a mess of the job? All the poles looked on line when I put them in. A week later, as I got ready to do the next row of poles, I took a different approach; I was working from the same corner pole, but this time the first pole I put in was not the next one down the line. Instead, I walked all the way to the end of the line and put the last pole in first. I put the second pole in only after I lined it up by looking over the corner pole to the last pole.

During my previous attempt, I did not put the last pole in until the very end. That was my mistake. The last pole needs to go in at the beginning, because you need it to sight all the poles in the middle. It meant more walking, because with each new pole I had to go back to the beginning and look to the end to see if the new pole was on line before digging the hole, but I had a straight fence line.

Now 13 years later, that first fence line is still crooked. I drove by it this morning. That fence line is a picture of my life. My life is crooked. Once the wire was up, it was too big of a hassle to pull the poles and set them straight. Locust poles last for 80 or 90 years so I imagine my grandchildren will be walking along that crooked line with their children.

The poles are like decisions I have made over the years. Those decisions are in the ground for good, some of them my grandchildren will see. For many years, I was working without the end pole in sight, thus the crooked line.

In the last page of my Bible, there is a verse that has become my end pole.

And they shall reign forever and ever.

As a follower of Jesus, I will be reigning with Jesus for millions and millions of years. After that, I will be reigning with Jesus for millions and millions more. The more I read the teachings of Jesus, the more I realize he had this post in sight when he was doing much of his talking. His fence line has no end, but he knows how far we can see.

One reason I have trouble keeping sight of the last fence post is because I have this obstacle called death impeding my sight. Jesus did not want this interruption to block our view, so he told us that his followers would not see death or even taste it. He said we will pass from life to life. If you were looking forward to some kind of death experience, I guess you will be disappointed.

Two years ago my family was in the room when my mother went from life to life. We saw half of the transition. We were with her singing one second, and one heartbeat later, she was free.

An hour or so later, I went for a walk down a street my mother had walked for 40 years. I remember thinking she may be walking with Jesus this very minute. Later in the Bible it says that to be absent from the body is to be present with the Lord. I know my mom was absent from her body. It was clear she just wasn't there anymore. She was with Jesus, and still is.

I am not sure why, but for years I allowed myself to have a very limited view of heaven. I thought of heaven as a long concert with amazing God music or a huge party at a beach house. I imagined seeing Jesus face to face. Part of seeing Jesus had a trip to the principal's office feel and part of it was like seeing a long lost friend. Oh, and I had this resting on a cloud bank picture in my mind.

To be honest, except for the seeing Jesus and other people part, I would have preferred to stay here in this life. I can go to concerts and the beach with friends right here so what's the hurry? As I dug a little deeper into my concept of heaven, I found a fear that I would become bored. Concerts can be great, but after four or five hours, I am ready to go home. I have been to great parties that have lasted all night, but never all week. A crash always came. Even the beach loses its appeal after a couple of weeks. I know seeing Jesus face to face will be incredible, but will I start to fidget after a few days/years/centuries?

Here's what I know. Jesus said he will never leave me or forsake me. He will be with me always. I also know he is coming back to earth in a very real, visible way sometime in the future. I hope to be alive when Jesus comes back, in which case, I will be in my present state for all the wild events described in the last book of the Bible. Otherwise, I will be with Jesus and lots of other people while events occur on earth.

After all the plagues, battles and glorious processions have come to pass, I will still be me only with an incorruptible body, living in the newly remade heaven and earth. The Jesus followers like me will not be dropped on Mars or housed on some cloud bank. We will be placed on earth with real water, trees, rocks, animals. There will be at least one city, Jerusalem, with streets. Each of us will have some sort of home or apartment. We will engage in wonderfully basic activities like eating and drinking.

God likes to keep what he has made and fix it up rather than throw it out. God likes water and air, light and land, sight and sound. He does not like the mess we have made of ourselves and his world, but he has not given up on either.

My corner pole is one day reigning with God on the recreated earth. I want to be ready. I like having lots of room to work and lots of projects to do. I get bored when my job description is too limited. It is a mistake to believe that all we have to do is get into heaven. We just went to the beach for a week. Kirsten and I did not stop our thinking at just getting inside the Bethany Beach town limits. We thought through meals, clothes, sun protection, movies for the car, rainy day activities, and beach toys.

Going to the beach for the week can still be wonderful even with no preparation, but sitting on the beach is more enjoyable if you remember to bring towels, bathing suits and chairs. It is entirely possible that you or I can be a follower of Jesus who has put more thought into family vacations than our eternal existence. To say it is all too much of a mystery to consider is not only incorrect, it's foolish. God wants us to live well for his glory and our good. He has given humans a capacity for vision. We can use our God given vision to line up our lives accordingly.

Normal people like you and me will be placed in positions of authority over certain aspects of God's creation. If you think about it, He has already given you authority of small areas of His universe. Does how I take care of our little farm have eternal significance?

Who we become during our remaining days does matter. My hope is that this book will help you become the kind of person who can enjoy the life God has given you now and enjoy an even fuller life in the years ahead.

Summary:

I have thought more about getting into heaven than about what I will do when I get there. Have you? I will be put I charge of some aspect of God's reign in the centuries to come, in part depending on how well I manage what I am in charge of right now.

Questions for discussion:

Describe a moment in your life when you experienced satisfaction over something you had created or accomplished.

Using the fence pole analogy, what is a decision someone could make that could make for a crooked fence line?

What is a decision someone could make in line with Jesus way of doing things?

What are some barriers to seeing yourself as ruling over part of God's Kingdom right now?

2
The Toy in the Cereal Box

I am not sure what you call it, but it ought to be removed from school playgrounds. It is a big flat disk with rails coming out from the center. Its function, I believe, is to separate the smaller children from the larger children through a spinning process. The smaller children start to slide away from the center and usually after a desperate attempt to hold on to the rail, end up being cast into the sand.

The earth is like that, only instead of a disk, we are on a spinning ball. God keeps it spinning and rolling through the universe at an alarming speed. All the while we mow our lawns, take our children to games and talk about the future; you know home improvements, college, and retirement.

If God decided, even just for a split second, to stop spinning the ball (Think of a basketball on a finger tip), we would all fly off into the ocean. Gravity is my reminder of God's goodness each day. It is an amazing provision. It is powerful enough to keep a truck in place yet not too powerful to crush a child. If the spinning ball scares you, the gravity cushion should help you feel secure.

In Christ Jesus we live and move and have our being.

Jesus holds it all in place. I would not trust anyone else.

It is not as if he came upon this ball bouncing through the universe and decided to pick it up and put people on it. He made the ball, gave it a spin, put human beings on the ball and said it was good.

Most days we do not think about the big ball and all the spinning, instead we focus on our own little worlds and that is often enough to grip our minds. We are finite creatures and I suppose our minds would snap if we knew too much. It is humbling, but it is also a gift.

Our dog does not know much. He has a pretty good life though. He has some concerns which are usually taken care of and his life is series of meals and naps. There are days when I desperately need God's perspective on my life. Sometimes it seems so challenging and difficult to manage.

It would help me to overhear God talk to someone else about my life. "Brian Donohue, he's got a nice life…he scurries about but from here it looks like a never ending stream of meals and naps. Every time I turn around, he is eating, just finished eating or talking about what he is going to eat and then he takes a nap, even if just got up 14 hours ago. I'd be bored living his life, yet he seems really challenged by it. He doesn't really do much but it sure tires him out. I watch his little brain try to workout all the future scenarios, he'll never have the intelligence to actually put it all together nor the power to make it happen, but he lives as if he is almost about to get it all under control. Thinking about his life tires him out more than actually living it."

I wonder how far I have drifted from the life God intended when he set Adam and Eve in the garden. I have had a few days in my life when I am so discouraged, it is like I cannot feel the sunshine, laugh or even taste the food I am eating. How much of that cloud covers all the other days? Why I am usually incapable of enjoying the present moment or of keeping a negative thought from detracting from the day? Why can't I wake up each day amazed at my ability to see or hear?

I know human sin has affected me and the world around me but I think we give the clouds more attention than they deserve most days. I am hopeless without God's light in my life. I have come to learn that I do not even have the capacity to enjoy the good days without God's help. You could ask me for my perfect day, work it all up and give it to me and I still might not be happy because something or someone did not go along with the plan. I am forever grateful that Jesus has made a way for me to go to heaven after I die, but I need help right now, today.

When I was 12 my dad took me to major league baseball game. One of my life's pursuits at that time was to catch a foul ball. I had attended games over the years and had never come close. Today looked to have real potential because of where we were sitting and for the first three innings my eyes were fixed on the game and my glove was ready. Along about the fourth inning, my mind began to zero in more and more on the need for a slice of pizza.

Instead of waiting for the break, I ran off in pursuit of my pizza. When I got back to me seat, the guy behind me showed me the foul ball he had just caught. He said it actually bounced on my seat, hitting my glove before he was able to grab it. That pretty much sums up my life.

I know that if I do not fix my eyes on Jesus, I will miss life, plain and simple.

When I was 4, the Murphy's came to visit. I liked the Murphy's and usually I was happy to hear they were coming, but not this time. You see, earlier in the week I had discovered the true secret to happiness and I did not want them to mess it up for me. My mom brought home a box of cereal and I realized that there was a prize inside. My mom told me I could have the prize, if it fell into my bowl during the normal course of pouring, and that could take some time. Now you know why I was nervous about the Murphy's visit.

Early Sat morning, my mom had set out a table for us in the kitchen and then went back to bed. I remember standing at the table working out my strategy. Kerry Murphy was my age and she was the one I was worried about. My little brother and Mike Murphy were only two, essential non-factors. I decided to go first...no prize. Deep breath, pass the box to Kerry...whew...no prize. Mike Murphy...no prize and finally on to my brother. I wasn't really worried about him because he was only two and if he got the prize, I was going to take it from him anyway. Still, no prize and we all started eating.

I was beginning to enjoy the day and was almost glad they were there when the unthinkable happened; Kerry Murphy stood up and said, "Hey there is a prize in the box". Then she shoved her little fist deep inside, fished around and pulled out the prize. I went crazy, I ran screaming into my parents room yelling, "She took the prize, she took the prize."

Even more shocking than the crime was my parent's response, they did absolutely nothing. The whole universe had been knocked off its ethical axis and they did nothing. How could human beings live like this, shoving their fists in? What happened to the "normal course of pouring"? What is truth? Am I now in a free fall? I can't say I found solid ground that day; years later I came to understand that the normal course of pouring was our family's approach to the toy in the cereal box.

We were at the Murphy's house one weekend and I got to see the Murphy's approach firsthand. When mama Murphy walked in the door from the store, the little Murphys grabbed the cereal boxes and pulled out the toys before the grocery bags reached the kitchen. Crazy though it seemed, I had to admit it was not immoral, it was just a different way of doing things.

Over the years, cereal boxes have become job opportunities and plastic prizes have become pop-up campers and screened in porches, but the story is the same. I am a little king who wants everything to go according to his will. If all goes according to my stated will, I may be happy or I may not because I might have thought of an additional preference in the meantime. You can bet I won't be happy if things do not go my way. I may be sad, mad, frustrated, hurt, spiteful, bitter and a whole host of other things, but I definitely will not be happy until my will is done.

You remember at the end of all things that Jesus wants his followers to reign with Him for ever and ever. Would you trust part of your universe to a guy who flips out over plastic toys in cereal boxes? Or stubborn printers?

Without God as my focus, I am an overgrown version of this child. The toys are more expensive but the child still wants his way. Without God, I honestly believe my personal happiness is the primary concern in the universe and only the constant expansion of my realm will bring happiness. I must continue to bring new toys, new tastes, new experiences and new understandings into my kingdom.

All those previously acquired items must stay where I put them in an orderly fashion, available at a moment's notice for my enjoyment. No vehicle is ever to need an oil change, no part of my house is ever to need repair and no relationship is ever in need of reconciliation. I have time only to expand my kingdom; I do not have time or energy to maintain any aspect of my kingdom.

My desire for happiness drives me onward into a bigger and bigger kingdom. I may start to get bitter and angry when I get older because my kingdom may start to shrink. Don't get too close to me then. Even as I am losing my grip on my own kingdom, I will still have eyes to see yours and I could try to use my words to try to diminish your realm until you are as miserable as I am.

Would you want to spend 5 hours on a plane next to a guy like that? Would you want to spend millions of years living next to him? If you were God, would you put him in charge of anything you actually cared about?

For some people, death is the last gift they will receive from God. Had they been allowed to live much longer, they would have become even more miserable people. Maybe in one way, death is an act of mercy, it stops the decline. After all, hell lasts forever, it is a 5 billion hour plane ride and the only one you are sitting with is yourself.

I am not sure how many more years I will have in this chapter on the spinning ball. I want to enjoy it and do what I was placed here to do. I know that God put in me a desire to reign and rule. I also know how miserable I can make myself and those around me if my focus is finding happiness only through expanding my own little kingdom.

Jesus I need your help. Teach me how to see life the way you see it. Grant me your perspective on my life, both its insignificance and its significance. Change me into someone who can rule and reign with you for the thousands of years to come.

Summary:

We all have little kingdoms we are ruling over all the time. We spend a great deal of energy expanding, defending and maintaining our kingdoms. Our happiness seems to be directly linked to how well things are going in our kingdoms at any given moment.

Questions for discussion:

How is gravity an expression of Jesus' love for us?

How would managing your kingdom be considerable more difficult if Jesus decided not to do the whole gravity thing tomorrow?

Can you share a story similar to the toy-in-the-cereal-box or the missed foul ball?

What are some aspects of your life right now that feel as important as the cereal toy?.

3
Pizza

Human beings have been perfecting the art of cooking for thousands of years now. The pinnacle was reached decades ago with the invention of Chicago deep dish pizza. All efforts now should be focused on production and distribution.

It was 8 at night and I was starving. I wanted deep dish pizza. I left my dorm room and was on my way to the car when I saw a friend and invited her to go with me. As I placed my order with the waiter, my friend made a request: could we put pesto on the pizza? I hesitated, trying to control my expression...Pesto on the pizza? What an abomination…deep breath…how about we put in on your half.

My mind was adjusting as the waiter walked away. I hate pesto and I would not have knowingly invited someone who wanted it in the pizza..?But it will work out...it will be only on her half. An hour later the pizza arrived. A mistake had been made; there was pesto in the whole pizza. The waiter said the chef made the mistake and we would not be charged for the extra pesto….What?….extra charge?…

I wanted a whole new plain pizza but it was too late, the restaurant was about to close. I tried to pick the pesto out. Finally I gave up and waited for my friend to finish, asked for a box and gave her the rest to take home for lunch the next day.

When I had left my room at 8, I had purposed in my mind to eat pizza…inviting a friend was an afterthought. In my kingdom, there is no pesto and the one who pays for the pizza chooses the toppings. I was clearly working within the accepted boundaries of my kingdom and yet my will had not been done.

Although I am modestly convinced that the world would run much better if everyone lived the way I do, I have come to accept that there are some legitimate variations. I no longer feel the need to help people see the wisdom of living my way and I have actually made some changes in my own kingdom based on what I have observed in others. But left to my own devices, I will try to orient those around me to true north in many subtle and not so subtle ways.

With other adults, it may come out in phrases like, "you might want to try....I used to do it that way but now...." . I have come to respect others as sovereign monarchs who have the right to rule over their own kingdoms the way they see fit, as long as their decisions do not create negative ripples into to my little part of the lake.

Our neighbor's child up the street likes to ride his motorcycle. Although I did not appreciate the ripple of noise that drifted into my world, I could deal with it. After a few weeks of this after school routine, my two year old developed a fear of the sound and screamed uncontrollably every time he got close to the house. If the ripple becomes a wave, I will have to deal with it.

Without Jesus as a focus, these little vignettes become our lives; a constant battle on a thousand fronts to ensure that our will is done in our own kingdoms and in the neighboring realms. After all, what is a good neighbor anyway; one who runs his kingdom more or less the way you run yours and is willing to help your will to be done on your side of the fence.

We were made with this innate desire to rule and reign. However, unless we learn to fix our vision on the final fence post, we will be like noisy geese honking at each other in the grass along the lake shore.

Jesus is the author and finisher of our faith. He is the one who made us and makes it possible for us to stay on the spinning ball each moment we live today. He did not set us here like fish in a pond and leave us to our own devices while he watches from above. He came to our world as one of us to teach us how to really live.

We can never talk enough about what Jesus did for us through his death on the cross. He died for me and every one else. Had he not paid the penalty for my sin, I would have no hope of a future life with God. I am grateful for regular communion services that remind me of that terrible cost he willingly paid for fools like me. As great a gift as his death was to humans, it was not his only gift to us. He came not just to show us a way through death...he came to show us the way through life.

For years, the cross was all I could think about when it came to Jesus. I missed so much. He did not come only to die on the cross for our sins. He came for many reasons, most of which I can not understand. I know this much, he came because he wanted to. I am quite sure he enjoyed much of his life: the feel of a warm fire, laughter with friends, the taste of good bread, listening to a good story and the peaceful feeling of lying down tired from a hard day's work.

He also came to teach us.

Jesus is the greatest teacher ever to walk the earth. He knew his audience, their fears, hopes and barriers to understanding. He knew they would learn best if taught through stories. People remember stories even if they are not ready to receive the instruction. The seeds of instruction are held inside the stories until the soil of the mind is ready to receive the truth. Stories can hold these seeds for years.

Knowing human beings to be like me, tripped up by pesto and motorcycle noise, he introduced the only truth that could set me free. Although you may think my first desire is for my will to be done, it runs deeper than that. I want to be happy. I am not expecting Christmas morning every hour for the rest of my life, but I am hoping for a consistent dose of satisfaction and enjoyment.

The most direct route in my mind is for my will to be done. But my direct route will not get me there. If I pursue my own will, I will never make it. I was not designed that way. I was designed to seek something else; the kingdom of God.

I have been telling you stories about the kingdom of Brian. It is where I live. You live in your kingdom where you are working to rule and reign. Jesus dropped a revolutionary seed into the garden of humanity. The seed was not well received, but it grew nonetheless.

We are not here to seek first our own kingdoms; we are here to seek first the kingdom of God.

God is like us enough to have his own kingdom, where things are done his way. Unlike my kingdom, which will leave little or no trace on the spinning ball after I go, his will last forever.

If a ten year old boy has a friend from school over for the first time, where will they go as soon as they come in the door? If the boy has his own room, they will go there. The visiting boy may walk around looking at things on the walls and shelves. If he starts to touch things, you would hear, "be careful, the glue is not very strong on that" or "that is an autographed baseball, I don't really like people to touch it."

After the tour is over they will settle down an engage in some activity. Set up games like Legos or army men have given way to computer games, but they all have this world with in a world idea. The boys are in the bedroom and not the living room because there they can govern themselves and until some need they cannot meet arises (usually hunger) they will not leave the room. Why? Because the host boy wants to run things according to his will without interference from family members. The boys have a better basis for their friendship if they have spent time in each other's rooms.

We get to know people by learning about their kingdoms. That is why visiting someone's home is so important. In our homes we display our kingdoms. Asking questions about pictures, books, furniture, landscaping, tools, cars, renovations and anything else you see will help you get to know someone. There is a certain amount of trust extended in the invitation to visit.

It may help you to think about your life in kingdom terms. What expansions do you wish to make? Are you looking to increase your kingdom through the acquisition of a new vehicle, computer or place to live? How much energy are you spending to maintain the kingdom expansions you have made recently? The second car can be huge help with moving the kids around. But it can also put strain on the budget and eat up time getting rides back and forth from the mechanic.

Maybe you expanded your kingdom to include more territory at work. There is satisfaction in the increase in influence, but all these extra meetings are eating up your time. Maybe you expanded your kingdom to include more activities for yourself or your children than you can maintain. I find that I do not leave enough margins in my life to manage well and enjoy what I have.

I am just learning why God put so many words into his requirements for a Sabbath day. Keeping the Sabbath is one of the Ten Commandments and God gives it more coverage than adultery, stealing and lying. God knows that we can spend our whole lives pushing for increase and never stop long enough to enjoy it all. Even at home, we can feel like there is too much to do to stop and read a book or play in the yard.

What drives you to expand your kingdom the way you do? Are you learning how to enjoy maintaining what you have acquired? Pulling clothes off the rack to purchase them can be fun. Why can't pulling those clothes out of the dryer to fold them three months later be just as fun? It is because we have believed the lie that happiness only comes from the expansion of our kingdoms and, with our access to resources, expansions are always at our finger tips. We should then be the happiest people ever to walk the earth. Well....are we?

Maybe it is not the particular expansion (car, clothes, relationships) that we seek. Maybe those things are just the wrappers. It is happiness that we are after and we think happiness is somehow tucked away inside those kingdom expansions. Most of them do have flavor, at least for awhile.

God made us to seek something outside of ourselves for satisfaction. He made us with a capacity for kingdom expansion and he wants to train us how to manage what we have. If we let Jesus teach us, we may very well live a joyful, meaningful life.

If instead we pursue the "he who dies with the most toys wins"mentality, we will find ourselves looking back one day at the crooked fence line that has become our life with deep regret. Life in all its flavor cannot be tasted by seeking first our own kingdoms. It just doesn't work that way. You can't get there from here. Only by learning to seek first the kingdom of God will you get what your heart desires.

Summary:

I want the world to run according to my will. When this does to happen, I get upset. I am convinced happiness will only come when I have an ever increasing kingdom where things go exactly the way I want them to. The universe simply cannot work if everyone has it running exactly the way they want it to. Only one person can have that privilege, that is the only way it will work. I am not that person and neither are you.

Discussion questions:

What is your version of the pesto in the pizza or the motorcycle on your street?

Describe a time when you have been able to catch yourself in the middle of acting really selfishly.

Describe a kingdom expansion that has brought you great joy?

Why is it easier to think of Jesus as Savior than it is to think of him as Teacher?

4
Faith like a Chicken

The first recorded public statement made by Jesus in the Bible is "repent for the kingdom of Heaven is at hand". Repent means to change direction, literally "turn around". We need to stop moving in the direction we are going: seeking to expand and maintain our own kingdoms and seek to expand and maintain God's kingdom instead.

There are road blocks we will immediately encounter if we are to make this change of direction.

Our first road block is our lack of ability to see the kingdom of God. God himself has chosen for us not to be able to see him right now. This could add to the difficulty, but it does not have to. If you think about it, I am invisible to you right now. I could be sitting next to you on a plane as you read this book and you would not know it. Yet, by this point in the book, you know a good deal about me.

You know I am married, lived in Chicago, have a farm in Virginia, grew up in Baltimore, and I like plain cheese pizza. We would have a lot to talk about if I introduced myself to you right now. But for now I am invisible. You may not think of me as having red hair, but I do. You know of some of my experiences, preferences and possessions. Before Jesus came to earth, pages and pages describing God's experiences, preferences and possessions were made available for people to read.

I look forward to seeing God face to face as Paul promises. I am more than a little nervous about the judgment part. As I get to know myself more, my desire for justice in the world has given way to hoping for mercy. In a way I am glad God chooses to keep our eyes from seeing him.

Imagine if God showed up tomorrow and stayed visible for the foreseeable future. Would you really be as focused on your personal kingdoms? Would you stay up late tonight talking about where to go to school or who to date or replacement windows if the God of the universe was visibly active outside? God is giving us a gift by remaining hidden to us.

He may be hidden, but God has allowed us a glimpse into his kingdom. Jesus said that unless you are born again, you cannot see the kingdom of God. Why is that? Before being born again, you do not have the capacity to seek any other kingdom than your own. You may hold the door for someone or even rush into a burning house to save a child, but at the core you are seeking your own kingdom.

You may not put these words on it, but you want to live in the kind of society where doors are held and children are saved so you are doing your part. We are still in essence doing things the way we want them done and hoping others will do likewise if the situation were reversed. Unless you die to your own preferences for the world, even the "good" preferences, you cannot see the kingdom of God.

A second road block we encounter is the fear that if we do not look out for number one, no one will.

Soon into his teaching, Jesus addressed this barrier in teaching about the flowers and the birds (Matt 6). We have chickens on our farm. Most days they are fed and watered but sometimes we forget to feed them. Yet every night, when the sun goes down, they go into the chicken coop and settle down for the night.

I have walked past the coop on the way to the wood shed many evenings and I have never overheard them pacing about wondering if it is all going to work out. They just go to sleep. They don't discuss amongst themselves the lack of food, nor calculate the likelihood of my forgetting to feed them again tomorrow. If is dark outside, they close their eyes and sleep. I am hoping to reach the level of faith demonstrated by these chickens.

In the winter, I tend to watch the evening news. It is May as I write this chapter and I have been too busy working outside for the last 6 weeks to bother with the news. The world is still one step away for disaster, I am just not thinking about the specifics. We just had this big swine flu scare. Last week people were freaking out about it. This week I see nothing on the front page of the paper at the gas station.

We humans freak out so easily. I want to become more like my chickens. Jesus' message to me is," Brian, do not worry about your life; the mortgage, braces, economy, health issues or car problems, look at the birds at the bird feeder and the yellow flowers in your pasture. I am able to keep them going; won't I do the same for you?"

Our family has lived for months at a time in the slums of a Mexican border town. I have known families that do not even have a cup or a spoon. Life is not easy for them by any means, but in general, they worry about fewer things than I do when I am living in the US. When I am living in the US, I have a tendency to worry about a lot. It all boils down to a concern that we will not be able to maintain a certain standard of living.

I have learned in Mexico that a couple of pallets, cardboard and sheet metal can make a house. And that you can live on beans and rice for a very long time. In the US, decisions need to be made about dentists and attic insulation, but it is a waste of my life to worry about these things. Most Americans could eat for a year by selling just the things they have in their homes.

You may be able to easily reconcile yourself to the first challenge of living with an invisible God. This second barrier of fear has a way of popping up anywhere, at anytime. This is why Paul encourages us to pray without ceasing. Our spiritual eyes will gravitate to our own kingdoms every time unless we train ourselves to fix our eyes on what is invisible (God).

Several years ago we left our farm in Virginia to begin a new ministry in Mexico. One of our biggest adjustments was leaving the blue and greens of Virginia for the brown on the high dessert. Our primary tree in the desert is a brown scrub oak and the landscape often looks burned over and dead. It works on you. Growing up on the east coast, I had grown accustomed to what I would call a certain level of mid-vision beauty. My own yard might not look so great, and it may be cloudy, but trees, rolling hills and pastures have color and appeal to them. In the desert, I cannot let my eye default to the mid-range vision. In the mid-range, it is all the same dismal brown. But if I look up, I see a beauty I rarely saw in the east.

At night there are stars so thick it looks like a white stone driveway and during the day the bright oceans of blue are gorgeous. I have taught myself to look up in the desert rather than out. Part of training ourselves to seek first the kingdom of God has to do with changing our focal point. The barrier of fear will diminish when we set our vision on God's kingdom. Only then will the aspects of our own kingdom be held in the proper perspective.

A third barrier to seeking the kingdom of God is our inability to get our minds around the concept of this kingdom God has. Jesus knew this would be a challenge, so he did what any great teacher would do: he built off the things his hearers could understand in order to help them step into what they couldn't yet grasp and he told stories, lots of stories.

People remember stories even if it is years before they can grasp the teaching contained within. Rather than list the attributes of the Kingdom, Jesus told us what the Kingdom was like: mustard seed, a pearl, a dragnet, a wedding, leaven, a vineyard owner, a small child, wheat in a field, seeds thrown in the ground..... Notice that all of these examples would have been readily understood by people in Israel at the time with access to farms and fishing.

I have no thought of summing up for you in a paragraph or a book what the creator of the universe took three years to teach, but I will point you back to the stories.

In my early years of following the way of Jesus, I allowed my mind to limit the gospel to some kind of eternal get out of jail free card. I said a sincere prayer acknowledging my own sin and belief in Jesus as my savior as a 20 year old, on August 6, 1986. I cannot say my moment of salvation did not come earlier than that, as I remember two or three moments of turning my soul toward Jesus as a child.

I would point back for sure to 1986 as the day I knew I had my eternal get out of jail free card. I envisioned dying one day. I could imagine Satan telling me I had to come with him and then pulling this card out of my pocket and saying "psyche, I am not going with you. I am going to heaven". I am still very happy to know I am going to heaven. However, I was wrong to think that when Jesus talked about his gospel or good news, he was only talking about my get out of jail free card.

Jesus did not come only to rescue me from hell, he came to lead me into his kingdom. Certain aspects of that kingdom will not be revealed on this side of death, but a whole bunch of it can be realized right here and now, if I will seek after it. I need the help of the Holy Spirit and those stories that Jesus told to even get started. My mind needs to constantly be renewed and recalibrated to seek God's kingdom and not my own.

There often seems to be a gravitational pull back down to the things of my kingdom and it takes effort to break free of that pull. Having to make that effort should not deter me from seeking his kingdom. Hardly anything worthwhile in this current realm can be achieved without effort (music, career, family, making a garden). God created the world that way, why should building a life around seeking his kingdom be any different?

Summary:

Jesus talked about his kingdom for three years. He made sure his followers remembered what he taught them so they could tell us. We can read the Bible and miss large aspects of Jesus' teaching on his Kingdom. We can get tripped up by the invisible nature of God's kingdom or by watching out for number one too much or by failing to look deeply into Jesus' description of the Kingdom of God.

Discussion questions:

Why do we need to change the way we think about life in order to hear Jesus' teaching on the Kingdom of God?

Why is being born again essential to seeing God's Kingdom?

Describe an aspect of your kingdom that is invisible to the group right now.

How can understanding the invisible nature of our own kingdoms help us accept the invisible nature of God's kingdom?

5
The Butting Order

Both my boys learned to ride bikes on the same day. As evening came, I was thrilled to see them ride around the circle without falling off their bikes. After those few minutes passed, a new fear entered my mind and stayed there for the next several weeks....what if they get hurt riding into each other? Does God have similar thoughts about his children?

The presence of other people has caused many a good man to wobble and crash on the path of life. Does Jesus know how complicated it gets trying to follow him with other people all around?

I am going to talk about a passage known as the Beatitudes. The approach I am taking is likely different from the one you have heard before, but I ask you to read along. The interpretation did not originate with me and I am not entirely sold on it, but it makes sense to me, so here goes...

Luke 6:20-26

> *Blessed are you poor, for yours is the kingdom of God.*
>
> *Blessed are you who hunger now, for you shall be filled.*
>
> *Blessed are you when men hate you, exclude you, revile you and cast your name out as evil, for the son of Man's sake.*
>
> *Rejoice in that day and leap for joy! Your reward is great in heaven, for in like manner their fathers did to the prophets.*
>
> *But woe to you who are rich, you have received your consolation.*
>
> *Woe to you who are full, for you shall be hungry.*

Woe to you who laugh now, for you shall mourn and weep.

Woe to you when all men speak well of you, so did their fathers to the false prophets.

In this passage you find several variations within two groups of people. One group seems to be on the low end of life and the other seems to have it made. The twist is that Jesus says the low group is the blessed or happy ones and the high group should be scared (Woe!). Now, either Jesus is completely out of touch with the way things really work in life, or he knows something we don't.

For many years on our farm we had angora goats. Within the herd there was a butting order. Each morning as I poured grain into the feed trough, a slightly varying drama would unfold, always with the same outcome. The number two or three goat would often arrive first and drive off any of the lesser goats until the number one goat arrived. She would start at the far end of the trough and run along it like a bowling ball scattering the others so she could eat in peace. Lesser goats could stand and starve for all she cared, and on larger farms, that can happen.

It can be amusing to watch the battles, if you are a human and above the fray, but it is life and death struggle for the goats. Happiness for a goat depends directly on her position in the butting order. They line up according to physical strength.

Human beings line up too. We are a little more diverse, but essentially the same. Goats line up according to how they rank in "body". Human beings can reach the top based on how they rank in not only "body", but also "brains" and "bank".

If I wanted to find the human butting order in any group of teenagers, I would go to the school cafeteria. This is often the only room in the school where students are allowed to choose their seats and if the school is large enough, the students will assign themselves tables based on their positions in the butting order. No adult needs to tell them this, they all do it automatically.

Think of what would happen if someone from lower down tried to sit at the popular table. Harsh words would serve in the place of the goat's horns but the affect would be the same.

Now back to the beatitudes. The poor, hungry, laughed at, where do they sit in the cafeteria? How about the well fed, popular laughing people, where do they sit? Which of these two groups would you call happy? Certainly not the ones at the bottom of the butting order.

Here's a modern version of the beatitudes just to get you thinking:

> *Happy are you who buy your clothes at Goodwill, for yours is the kingdom of God.*
>
> *Happy are you who have nothing for dinner tonight, for you shall be filled.*
>
> *Happy are you when people at school or the office make fun of you for believing in Jesus or mock you for not getting involved in the gossip.*
>
> *Jump up and down like your team just won the Superbowl, because the parents of those people harassing you did the same thing to the godly people who lived before you.*
>
> *Sad are you who buy only expensive clothes from the top designers, strips of cloth are all you will ever have.*
>
> *Sad are you who eat out at fancy restaurants every evening, it's mac and cheese from here on out.*
>
> *Sad are you who get all the attention from the guys when you are out on the town, your mascara will run with tears of rejection.*
>
> *Sad are you who now run with the popular crowd, there are many tormented souls in hell who were just like you before they died and found out they weren't "all that".*

In Jesus day it was a common belief that God loved the people with more brains/body/bank than those with less. When Jesus said to the disciples, "it is easier for a camel to go through the eye of a needle than for a rich man to enter the kingdom of God", his disciples were stunned. "Who than can be saved?" they asked.

In other words, we all know that God loves the ones at the top of the butting order more than the ones at the bottom. If the ones at the top can't get in, what chance do we have? "With God, all things are possible" Jesus replied.

You are not your position in the butting order. This is really good news, no matter where you fit on the human scale.

There once was a junior in a small rural high school who had been the leading scorer on his basketball team for three years running. He walked down the middle of the hallway at school and talked as loud and as often as he wanted. His dad signed him up for a summer camp in June where he played with college level players and significantly improved his play with his left hand.

In August, his dad got transferred to Chicago and the local high school had a nationally ranked team. Both father and son were excited about the potential NCAA exposure as the tryouts began. Unfortunately the boy was not good enough to play regularly; they only put him in when the team was up by more than 25. The coach did not want him in there when the games were close, he was nice kid and all, but he simply wasn't good enough to be out there. Do you think the boy talked loudly and walked down the middle of the hall anymore? Did he laugh as often as the year before?

He was actually a better ball player than he was after his junior season; the only thing that changed was the group of people surrounding him. We must not get caught seeing ourselves through the lens of the human scale. This human butting order is only maintained through constant comparison and competition. It does not give us an accurate reflection of who we are.

The poor person Jesus talks about is not happy because he is poor. There are certain benefits to having small kingdoms: you do not have much to lose or maintain, but generally it is not a pleasant existence. The transient families we see come through our neighborhood in Mexico without a spoon or cup do not have a long worry list but they are not laughing a whole lot either. It is naive to say poverty leads to happiness.

Many of those who have chosen to live with less find joy in it, but they know they can go back to a higher standard of living if they want to. The destitute people we see along the border have no option for stepping out of the poverty anytime soon. Yet I have seen people in extreme poverty living meaningful, joyful lives, not so much because of the absence of material possessions, more so because of the presence of the kingdom of God in their lives.

In the section we call the beatitudes, I believe Jesus is highlighting the people at the bottom of the human scale in order that everyone, no matter what their allotment of brains/body/bank/ sees a pathway to the joyful life found only in living a life centered on seeking first the kingdom of God, today, right now. We do not have to wait until after we die to get started, that would be a stupid thing to do.

We each need to decide how we are going to take Jesus' teaching. Is Jesus saying that we should never eat a full meal or laugh? Is he saying that only poor people can enter the kingdom of God? Or is he speaking about the extremes of humanity in order to teach all of us? I believe his point here is that the kingdom of God is available to all regardless of your position on the human scale.

If poverty is measured, the poorest American would still be classified among the rich of the world today. If the kingdom of God is only available to the poor, will there be any Americans in heaven? I have been known to laugh at a funny story on occasion. Am I now destined to an eternity of mourning and weeping?

I do not believe Jesus is telling us here that his kingdom is only available to the poor-hungry-crying-hated people. If those were the only requirements, I could make myself a poor-hungry-crying-hated person and still have no interest in God. Would I still receive the kingdom of God because I met the requirements?

Nor is Jesus telling me he wants me to avoid buffets and laughter. I believe Jesus is describing how life usually is among humans. The people at the top of the butting order sure look a lot happier on the magazine covers than the people with less who are waiting in the check-out line. Jesus offers an invitation for a whole new kind of life. One that is not limited to the rich, poor or anyone in between.

If you are a human, and you put your trust in the person of Jesus, you are in. The human scale is just the background. God can do marvelous works in you and through you at any seat in the cafeteria. You have to be willing to do things his way and you will soon see he truly does know what he is talking about.

Summary:

In our world, happiness seems to come from having more brains/body/bank than those around us. If we build a life around moving up the human butting order, we cannot have the life Jesus offers us right now. It just won't work. The Human scale was just as real 2,000 years ago as it is today. Each one of us in one way or another needs Jesus to set us free from this trap so we can live life in the Kingdom now.

Discussion Questions:

How have you seen the human butting order play out in your life?

What signs are there in your world that people of all ages are seeking to move up in the order?

How did you find the paraphrase of the beatitudes to be helpful?

Why was it so important for Jesus to remove this lie (the human butting order) from the minds of his listeners at the beginning of his teaching years?

6

The World is Flat

Imagine you are Christopher Columbus. You know the new world is just across the ocean and you would go alone tomorrow if you could. But you cannot sail the boat by yourself. You go from pub to pub, town to town, trying to talk sailors into going with you. You paint glorious word pictures of the land they will be the first to see. You talk of gold and riches, fame and adventure. Many turn away, but a few hear you out. Of those few you always get to the same point....and then their faces go blank and you lose them. "Where is this new land?" they ask. "We will find it by sailing west for as far as the eye can see." Yup, you lost them. They start finishing their beers and get up from the table.

No matter what picture you paint of this new world, it doesn't matter. You just can't get there from Europe. Every sailor knows that just as the sun rises in the east, if you sail far enough west, you will fall off the earth.

Jesus knew that all his descriptions of the kingdom of God would fall on deaf ears, unless he dealt with the lies in the way. It was a lie that the world was flat. No person today would believe it. But we believe other lies.

We believe that the good life really does come from moving up the butting order through investing in brains/body/bank. We believe that we should be constantly scanning our horizons for new topics to worry about. Parents especially think they are required to engage in this practice not only for themselves but for their children daily, if not hourly. Isn't that what parental love is all about? Or is it? After all, we can write checks and make choices; shouldn't that combination make the spinning ball (earth) safe for our children?

It is a lie that what you see is all there is. Jesus dealt with these lies, and many others, as he presented his kingdom message. Think of the kingdom message as a plant Jesus wants to put in a garden. Each generation has its own set of lies constantly, albeit slowly, surfacing in the garden of the mind. Some lies are rocks that need to be dug up and tossed out. Maybe the lie about the human scale is one of those rocks.

Other lies are more like weeds that creep back in over and over again. Fear is more like these weeds; you can pull clumps out in the beginning, but you better keep checking for them every day or they will take over.

As Jesus is clearing the garden of the "world is flat" rocks and weeds, he is also planting his stories in the soil of our minds.

Our farm house was built around 1900. Life was very different for those first residents and a large change was coming with the invention of the automobile. If I were able to walk through some time portal and join them for dinner, how would I explain to them life with an automobile? How many of you would have drastic changes in your employment, education, entertainment and social lives if all the cars in the world were somehow removed tonight? Picture me at the kitchen table trying to prepare them for the new life. I could say a car was like a wagon with its four wheels. I could say it's powered like a train and that you steer it with a smaller version of a ship's wheel. This would help them to recognize what Henry Ford would soon be talking about.

Jesus does the very same thing with his stories about the kingdom of God. When he says it is like a mustard seed, he is describing one aspect of the kingdom, just as the image of a wagon emphasized the general size and shape of a car. The kingdom of God is like a mustard seed in that it does not look like much at the beginning. But if you let this seed grow within you, it can change the world.

I have seen families radically changed as the father begins to take in Jesus' teaching. Certain sinful, selfish activities start tailing off and his interests shift to bring more life to the family. It is a slow process, with ups and downs, but with each daily choice to live Jesus' way, the family changes for the better. It may not look like the plant is actually growing for days or an even months at a time, but it is.

If you look though the gospels, especially the book of Matthew, you will see Jesus say over and over again, "the kingdom of God is like….a pearl, a dragnet, a seed, a wedding."

Jesus says the Kingdom of God is like weeds coming up in a field of wheat. This explains why God allows evil to continue along side good. Along the Mexican border the drug cartels are particularly active right now. Could God destroy them? Sure, but it would likely wipe out people like me who are trying to help others learn about Jesus.

It will all get sorted out in the end. I do not need to worry it. I need to keep my eyes fixed on doing what I can to point people to Jesus through caring for people he cares about. Our children's soup kitchen is a place of light in this neighborhood. As this ministry grows in strength and influence, so are the drug gangs. Both will likely grow larger in the years to come.

Jesus says the Kingdom is like a treasure hidden in a field. A man sells all he has and buys this field. When I was junior in college, I remember sitting in my business classes, dreaming about what it might be like to make a lot of money. During the summer between junior and senior year I responded clearly to Jesus' invitation to follow him.

I went back for my senior year with an entirely different mentality. I was more interested in books about Jesus, than the Wall Street Journal. I was more interested in people than my grades and I had a new desire for my life to be pleasing to God rather than just pleasing to myself.

During the middle of my senior year, I decided to apply for a 6 week summer missions project in Costa Rica. From December until April I waited for an acceptance letter. Meanwhile, I interviewed for jobs and I was offered a great one in a bank management program in my hometown of Baltimore. The only hitch was that it was due to start a week before my internship in Costa Rica was scheduled to end. I tried to contact the missions leaders to see if I could leave early.

I was still waiting for an answer when the VP from the bank called wanting a definite answer. I took a risk and chose the treasure in the field. I told the VP I wanted the job, but if starting on time was a requirement, then I would have to decline. I could tell by the silence on the other end of the line that we were in uncharted waters. He said he'd call me back.

That night I went to a senior dinner and saw one of my professors there. He asked me how the job hunt was going. I told him I had a great offer and I also told him of my latest conversation with the VP. I remember this professor as kind of a grumpy hard-nosed business man and so I was surprised when his face lit up as he said "even if you lose this job because of your trip to Costa Rica, you'll never regret it".

Encouragement came from an unexpected person that night. It all worked out, but later I was glad for what it did for my soul to have to make the choice. I will never forget hearing my own voice say I would rather give up this job I had been working toward than miss the opportunity go to Costa Rica. At 21 years old, I had learned how to sell all and go for the kingdom.

The kingdom of God is also like a wedding banquet. I like weddings. I especially like receptions with good music, lots of food and a large dance floor. I like evening weddings because people do not make plans for afterward and many will stay late. Kirsten and I love to dance and wedding receptions are our only opportunity these days.

In some cultures wedding receptions are brief affairs. I call them the "Here's a sandwich for the ride home" variety. In other cultures wedding receptions are the take a nap earlier in the day so you can stay up late dancing kind and I like those the best. Jesus first recorded miracle in the book of John is his turning the water into wine. There are many good reasons for refraining from the use of alcohol, but our opinions on the subject may cause us to miss the gift of Jesus here.

Several grooms have told me their main fear is that their reception would be boring and that people would leave early. No one wants their wedding to be remembered as the boring one. In many cultures, when the wine runs out, the people start leaving early and this was about to happen to this poor couple. Jesus apparently did not want to perform this miracle initially; he knew it would push him into his more public ministry.

Perhaps he was leaning against the wall, tapping his feet to the music or maybe sitting at a table laughing and telling stories with his friends. Maybe he was out dancing when his mother came up and asked him to solve the problem. We do know that once he started performing miracles, his days of enjoying being one of the crowd were over.

I am sure there were many moments of being a human that Jesus positively enjoyed and those moments were about to become few and far between once he became a public figure. Even his mother did not know what it would cost him to do this little miracle. If she had seen it as the first step to the cross, I doubt she would have asked him. But she did, and he stepped into to keep the party going.

I am not surprised that the wine tasted good. I can't imagine Jesus making bad wine. The master of the feast was surprised at the good stuff coming out at the end. I remember in our fraternity that the good beer, the kegs of Lowenbrau, came out at the beginning of the party and after mid-night we started rolling out the kegs of Blatz. By then everyone was too far gone to know the difference.

If Jesus knew how to keep the party going here on earth you can bet he can throw a good one in heaven. I do not want to miss it. The kingdom has an invitation to it and each of us needs to decide what to do with it. If you have never been to a good reception or you don't like dancing, laughing and eating great food, you can stay home and watch TV. The bride and groom will most likely not come and forcibly remove you from your living room. There will come a time when it will be too late to respond to Jesus' invitation to the kingdom banquet. What would you rather being doing instead?

The kingdom of God will be first and foremost a party, not just because of the food and the music, but because of who will be in the room.

Summary:

Your happiness does not depend on your allotment of brains/body/bank. Your happiness does depend on how much of Jesus' teaching you allow to govern the way you live. Jesus told stories and made analogies because that is how humans remember truth. Stories with truth wrapped inside can stay with us for decades. If we cannot receive the lesson at the time of the teaching, it still stays inside the story. Years later the story may open up in your mind like a flower and the truth comes out. You may think, "that's what my Grandfather was trying to tell me." Jesus told lots of stories about the kingdom of God so we could digest them and always have them with us.

Discussion questions:

How have you seen people suffer from the human scale based on brains/body/bank?

Can you share about a time when you allowed worry to creep in and rob your joy?

Today, we may not believe the world is flat, but we believe other lies about life, what are some of them?

When you hear the story of Jesus at the wedding, what strikes you the most?

7

Unleaded Only

Jesus tells us what the kingdom is like (mustard seed, pearl, wedding banquet) so that we can recognize it and respond to the invitation. Much of his teachings describe the way one lives in this new kingdom. There are some aspects of the kingdom I will not experience until after I die. But I believe it is a mistake to think that whenever Jesus teaches, he is talking about life after death. I have no doubt that a dramatic change will come when I die, but I do not have to wait that long.

Death always precedes change. I must die to my need to have everyone like me before I can change into a leader God can use. I must die to my need to always be right before I can change into a person who can have a happy marriage. I must die to my desire to "have it my way". If I don't, God will not change me into the kind of person who can seek first his kingdom.

In the early chapters of this book there were lots of stories about little human kingdoms, mostly in reference to my own. On one level, I told those stories so that you could get a vision for yourself as a king or queen of a realm. Your realm contains all that you have say over. In simple terms, your emotions are like hospital machines describing the level at which your will is being done within your realm.

If you are irritated or frustrated, usually a management issue has surfaced in your realm and you don't like it. Our vacuum is never supposed to break down; in fact nothing mechanical that I paid money for is ever supposed to break down. The mercury on my irritation/frustration level shoots up when I have to stop and deal with a broken machine.

My children are supposed to behave and be grateful, at all times or my annoyance/anger meter starts rising. Never mind the countless memories of my own childhood behavior, my kids are not supposed to be that way. If I am bored, it often means that the days, weeks and months ahead stretch out before me like a long flat kingdom maintenance desert. I do not see any opportunities for expanding my kingdom to include new purchases, experiences or friendships. Life looks like a never ending stream of Mondays and I am depressed.

If I am satisfied, usually that means I tried something new in my kingdom and it is going according to my will. The new truck runs well, the game looks great on the new TV, the team I have decided to root for is actually winning, the children are enjoying the new sandbox, the new recipe tasted really good.

If I am feeling jealous, maybe I am looking over the fence at a neighboring kingdom and wishing I could have that riding mower too. If I am feeling frustrated, it often means that my attempts to expand my kingdom have been thwarted or delayed. The money we had been setting aside to buy an outdoor grill was needed to repair the transmission or the prerequisite class for my major is not offered this semester, pushing my graduation back a year.

You do not need to act on your emotions.

If I feel a set of teeth bite into my leg, pain will shoot up to my mind telling me to react quickly. In one case I will kick the owner of the teeth and in another case I will do nothing. The first case is a neighborhood dog and the second is my two year old daughter. Emotions are a gift to us; they speak to us about the status of our kingdoms. We ignore them or indulge them at great cost to our souls. We need to learn how to interact with them the way Jesus would if he were in our shoes.

If you can see your own personal kingdom, you can begin to have a framework for someone else's kingdom. God is someone else and he has a kingdom that he wants you to see. If you can recognize that your kingdom is for the most part invisible, you can handle that fact that God's kingdom is largely invisible too.

There is another benefit to all this talk about personal kingdoms. If we can keep the final fence pole of reigning one day with Jesus firmly in our minds, we will see our moments at the mechanic shop or in the check out line at Wal-Mart as part of our fence. How would Jesus want me to think about the slow cashier? Are moments in the check out line excluded times from walking with Jesus? I have found that I pay more attention to God when things do not go my way. Right now I do have things I am in charge of. If God came into my kingdom today to have a walk around what would he say?

Are there things/habits/attitudes/relationships he would tell me to get rid of? Would he disapprove of the way I am speaking to certain people in my kingdom or how I am thinking about someone or something? Would he tell me to spend less time focused on one aspect and more on another? This life is my chance to grow into the kind of person who can be trusted with part of God's kingdom in the years to come.

How am I doing with what I have right now? If I drove up to rent your house in a car so full of trash that you could not open the doors with out major spillage, would you trust my promise to keep your house clean? If I do not treat the people around me well right now, do you think Jesus will put me with other eternal beings years from now or would I be better suited for a heavenly Alaskan weather station?

In John 14, Jesus says that if we keep his commandments (manage our kingdoms the way he would) he and his father will come and make their home with us. Have you ever gone to stay at a house that was managed in such a way that you wanted to leave early? Odds are that if the host knew you were going to feel that way, they might have made some changes beforehand. Jesus is standing at the door of my personal kingdom, knocking.

Jesus says that every one who is fully trained will be like his master. I want to be like my master. I want to be like Jesus. Jesus handled everything that came at him in a way that pleased his father. I want to live that way too. When I think of myself, I think of the failures nine times out of ten, but I will give you a positive example to get us going.

I was working in a corporate office at the time. It was first thing one morning when my boss came over and said, "Brian clear your desk and work only on this lease project. I need it right away." Twenty minutes later she came back and said, "Here is a budget project I need by lunchtime". So I worked on the second project for the next few hours.

Just before lunch, she walked up and asked me if I had completed the first project. When I said "no, I have been working on the budget project", she started yelling at me in front of the whole office and then walked out to go to lunch. While she was gone, I stayed at my cubicle and worked on the first project. The whole office heard what had happened and there were lots of looks and comments encouraging me to "tell her off".

I certainly had clear grounds for my case and lots of willing witnesses. But then I thought about what Jesus says when someone sins against you. He says that you should first talk to the person privately, then take a witness or two, and only after those steps don't work, let the group hear about it. Man's way of dealing with it would have been to tell her off where people could hear it; God's way was to deal with it privately.

When she walked in from lunch, I asked her if we could talk for a minute in the conference room. I told her that for the most part I liked working for her but this morning I did not. I went over what happened saying that I cannot do two things at once and that I was only doing what she told me to do. She said, "Well my boss did the same thing to me about those two projects. He wants them both immediately." Then it grew quiet, and I let it stay quiet....finally she said, "I did not like it when my boss did that to me, so I guess I should not have done that to you." That was as close to an "I'm sorry" as we were going to get so I thanked her and went back to my desk.

Human beings love to be offended. It gives us strange warmth and a twisted joy inside. We even get joy out of being offended for other people. Is that what God wants? He wants us to be peace makers and I know my actions that day did bring a measure of peace to that office. It did not give my coworkers as much to talk about as "telling her off" publicly would have, but we are supposed to provide an example, not entertainment.

When I took that job at the bank I told you about just out of college, I went and bought a new black Ford Ranger pick-up truck. I remember washing it in our driveway on a bright sunny day. The car sparkled just like the commercials. It occurred to me that this truck was really mine. If I took good care of it, I could have it for years. Since I did not know much about cars, the owner's manual was very important to me.

I could have poured orange juice in the gas tank, and the Ford motor company was not going to say a thing. But if I wanted it to run well, I'd better stick to their recommendation of unleaded gasoline. God's commands are like that owners manual. You can pour orange juice in your gas tank if you want to, but you won't run very well. If you want to run as you were designed to run, you'd better stick to the manufactururer's recommendations.

A few years back I was flying in a plane from Germany to London. As I took my seat at the window, a 25 year old girl from Czechoslovakia sat next to me followed by a 20 year old guy from California. The guy had a Jim Beam bottle full of a drink he mixed himself and the two of them had been working on the bottle in the waiting area. This was a Ryan Air flight, so there were no seat assignments, flight attendants or rules. You could bring your own drinks.

The guy was on his way home after a two month tour of Europe chasing women and experimenting with drugs and alcohol. She was on her way to England to stay with a friend. She had to leave she said, because she had been sleeping with two different guys for months now and she could not take the pressure anymore of living a double life. The guy listened to her story and offered a solution; she should come to California and live with him. They chatted about some of the details, until he said, "I'll give you my e-mail address when we land" and got up to go to the bathroom.

She then turned to me and asked me about my life. I told her about our work in Mexico and she asked me if I really believed the Bible. She was not mocking me but she looked at me as if I believed in the Easter Bunny. She told me that none of her friends back home believed anything about Christianity and how strange it was to actually talk with someone who lived based on Christ's sayings.

There was a pause and then she said, "Well, you heard my situation, what do you think?" I said, "God did not design you to have sex regularly with two different people. Sex is more than just the experience in the moment, something more is going on, it is a soul connection of the two people and God set that up for husband and wife only. If you live differently than God intended, it's not going to work".

At this point the guy came back and they started talking again but I could tell she was in a whole different frame of mind. In a few minutes he got up and sat in the seat one row up and began talking to the two girls in front of us. We heard him say to one of the girls, "You should move to California and live with me". The Czech girl smiled and I said," I wouldn't wait around for that e-mail address if I were you."

We then had a great conversation of Jesus. You see, she had tried pouring orange juice in her gas tank. Had she obeyed Jesus commands about sex, she would not have been so miserable. The more we talked, the more she smiled. She was finding her way again and was very thankful for our conversation.

She was not ready to trust what Jesus had to say about the next life just yet, but she sure believed he knew what he was talking about when it came to relationships in this life. If people are willing to try some of Jesus' advice for managing their personal, day to day kingdoms, they will find that it works. Jesus does know what he is talking about.

Your own little kingdom is the main place where you and Jesus can spend time together right now. You can't go to his house just yet, but he can come to yours. There is only one drawback, when he comes in; he tends to tell you what to do. This can make you mad at first until you try out some of his suggestions. After awhile you will learn that his way is best. You will find that the peace and joy you have so long desired does not come by orienting your life around your preferences, but by regularly saying, "Not my will but yours be done".

Summary:

Your emotions are like an instrument panel for your soul. They gauge the level at which your will is being done in your personal kingdom. God gave emotions to us and we need to learn how to live well with them. Also, when we engage in ways of thinking, speaking or acting contrary to Jesus' way, our lives will not run smoothly. No human is exempt from suffering and disappointment. However, the only hope we have for a good life flows out of regular decisions to manage our kingdoms the way Jesus would if he were king in our place.

Discussion questions:

Can you think of a time when someone you know made a personal kingdom management decision in accordance with Jesus' teaching?

Can you describe moral decision someone could make that would be the soul equivalent of pouring orange juice in the gas tank?

How will incorporating Jesus' teaching into your way of life now, prepare you for the age to come?

8
Rolling Joints

When I was sixteen I had a job as a busboy at a steak and lobster restaurant. After we closed at night, the waiters often went to parties and sometimes I went along. I had been around people smoking marijuana before but these parties were my first opportunity to really see how the joints were made. I could not figure out why they were making them so small. Besides the manual dexterity required for the task, the end result left such a tiny air passage, I was sure blood vessels were about to burst with each inhale. The strain resulted in quite a comical expression. It was hard not to laugh.

When I catch myself looking for praise from other people, I remember those friends. In those moments I am trying to inhale glory through a joint, hoping for some kind of high. I am not sure but I think other people are like that too. Maybe I am fishing for a compliment about something I have made, or the behavior of the children or laughter over something I have said. The joint seems always right at hand and I am quick to take a hit.

Jeremiah wrote about 600 years before Jesus showed up and he talked about the marijuana joint. He did not use those words, but he meant the same thing. He warned people not to glory about how smart they are, how rich they are or how strong they are. He said, "If you want to glory (or brag) about something, brag that you know God and that you know what he likes."

It is the same brains/body/bank thing from a couple of chapters back. Basically, human beings try to take hits of glory off recognition they receive from other people. The glory hit comes because one person has slightly more brains/body/bank/ than the average person. The body people show up on magazine covers and sometimes the bank people join them.

The brains people don't usually get the press but they can take their hits talking with friends about the stupidity of lower downs or about how they have outsmarted the system (investments / purchases / interpersonal victories).

You can even roll your joint in the form of a prayer request, "Please pray for me, I have three excellent job offers and I am not sure which to choose". Or "pray for me, this great looking guy really likes me and I don't know how to tell him I am not interested." Some people know how to use their periphery vision to take hits from people turning to look at them in public places. This version is a quick low level buzz since one can't really stop and take it all in, but a series of them in a row can give you a rush.

You may be an excellent cook who rolls a joint by saying to your friends, "I wish I could cook as well as so and so, I am such a klutz in the kitchen". Then you wait for your friends to put some weed on the table in the form of, "your such and such dish is the best I have ever had, or remember last week when you brought your whatever and people would not stop talking about it." After a few such comments you actually need a little break so you can roll the joint and take the hit, too many good compliments in a row and you're bound to forget some of them.

It starts early in life. In school, if you do well on a test, you are not supposed to just announce it, marijuana joints aren't supposed to be rolled in plain view. You have to be more subtle. You ask your friend, who you know did not do so well, "How did you do?" ... "I got a 71" your friend pauses trying to escape from the moral obligation before finally giving in and saying..."How did you do?" You then respond, "I messed up, I missed one, I only got a 98" Joint rolled, hit taken, now let's go to the hallway and look for more weed.

You can get addicted to this stuff. You can never get enough glory from people no matter how much power you have at work or how often people admire you for your children. It's a bad habit and God knows you are doing it.

The Bible says we are not to glory from brains/body/bank but rather in knowing God. If I am the one with the most bank in the group and I brag about it, you may not like it but you know it is true. How much more arrogant would I be if I walked around saying, "yup, the infinite, eternal God of the universe, I know him".

We have all heard people brag about knowing a famous person. It can be irritating but that's nothing compared to a human coming out and saying he knows God. Yet this is what Jeremiah encourages us to do, to find our glory not in our comparative allotment of brains / body / bank, but in knowing the God of the universe. Jesus came along later and summed up eternal life not as the heavenly Disneyworld without pain and lots of food, but as knowing God.

When I was younger, I was not so sure about the God of the Old Testament. I could relate to Jesus, but the Old Testament God sounded harsh to me. It wasn't until recently that I got a better perspective on it.

Suppose you are a 20 year old coming to stay with our family for two months. As soon as you walk in the door, our three year old marks the wall with a crayon and I send him to his room until morning, no dinner, no good night story, nothing. As you stand in the doorway with your suitcase, you might be thinking, "Brian seemed really nice when I heard him teach, but he seems like a totally different person at home, I think I made a mistake in coming here."

Now imagine a slightly different variation of the same story, you are still 20 only now you are at the end of your two months with us, the child makes his mark on the wall and gets sent to his room just the same. The only difference is that two months ago, you saw the beginning of this crayon on the wall drama.

On day one, mark on the wall, "please don't do that"…

five marks later "I wish you would not do that"…

Ten marks and two days later, "if you keep going, it's time out for you."….

3 marks later "That's it, you are in time out for 30 seconds"…

5 days and 20 marks later we are up to five minutes of time out when I get drastic…."one more mark and I am taking your crayon away".

Mark….and I take the blue crayon…the child picks up a red crayon and we start all over again for ten days….then a yellow crayon…

Now fast forward to your last night with us, the house is covered in crayon marks and then you see me send the child to his room for the night. What do you think of me now? "It is about time....I can't believe you waited this long, I would have screamed at the kid weeks ago...you are the most patient person I have ever met." What changed in this scenario?

The only thing that changed was when you walked in on the scene. Now your impression of me is entirely different, not because of what actually happened, but because of when you began observing. Most of the time we walk in on God and his children in the Old Testament, they are about to put that final mark on the wall.

The same wisdom applies in assessments we make of other people....we know far less than we think. We are blind to 95% of the challenges they are having managing their kingdoms right now, we only see a little bit and how quick we are to make snap kingdom assessments.."If I were that guy, I would tell her she can...." Or if that were my child I would...." Usually it is better to talk to God in prayer for the person in a kingdom management crisis than to offer your pearls of wisdom.

What can we know about God? He is a person like us in some ways and a lot depends on how much he chooses to show us about himself. We all act differently depending on who is around. The less we trust or know the people around us, the less we reveal of our personal kingdoms.

You learn in grade school to be careful what information you share about your kingdom to even one person. You may still like building with Legos, but you better not let word get out unless you are sure that Legos are still "cool", you might get labeled as playing with baby toys. One or two times getting burned is usually enough to teach children to be careful to whom they tell their secrets, especially about which boy or girl they like.

We learn to be careful about sharing our career goals with our bosses or sharing our struggles with our neighbors....people talk you know. God does not let us see his entire kingdom right now. If we saw too much of his kingdom right now, we might gain knowledge of him; knowledge we could not handle in our current state.

You may have changed your opinion about a co-worker after visiting his house or apartment. The more of someone's kingdom we see, the more we know them. Fame is expensive, you do get more glory hits from people, but perfect strangers feel like they have a right to talk about your personal life in the grocery store. God hides his kingdom too. He says you can't even see it until you are born again. In one aspect, being born again is going from a person who seeks his own kingdom, to becoming a person who seeks God's kingdom. In other words, God does not want to let anyone in who has a separate agenda. The price at the door is dying to yourself. It is a steep cost unless you consider that you can't keep your life forever anyway. You had better lay it down now when there is the opportunity for a better arrangement.

Knowing that God cared enough for glory addicts like me to come teach us how to live well and then die a painful death for our failures...well...that's all the information I need to want to get to know him more. But he gave us so much more to go on.

Paul tells us we can know God through his creation. I have seen some beautiful places in my life. Right now I am in thinking of this white sand beach in Venezuela that curved below a gorgeous mountain range. Sunshine glittered off the waves and beautiful trees swayed with the breeze that blew off the ocean. Imagine how happy I would be if I could open my closet door and step into that scene anytime I wanted to.

Or maybe for you it is 10 inches of powder on a still, sunny day at a ski slope in the Rockies with a hot tub waiting at the bottom of the hill. As the sun set last night I looked out over our farm. The grass was freshly cut, beneath the maple tree bursting with leaves, my children rolled on the ground laughing with the puppy I brought them. I stood by the picket fence smelling the honeysuckle with a deep sense of satisfaction. I would have been happy to have viewed this scene anywhere, but it was especially enjoyable knowing the role I had in setting it up.

Imagine the joy God has when people are engaged in wholesome activities in the thousands of beautiful places he has created. Imagine how awesome it will be to be with God when he creates the new heavens and the new earth.

I thought of Jesus as loving and creative, but I did not always think of him as smart for some reason. I guess I focused too much on his sacrificial death and not enough on what he said.

One of my favorite recorded interactions is when he was challenged by the religious leaders over paying taxes to Caesar. They were trying to trap him. "Is it lawful to pay taxes to Caesar?" they asked. If he said "yes", they were ready to jump on him for loving Rome, thereby turning the people against him. If he said "no", then they were going to report him to the Roman officials. Instead, he said.. "Give me a coin.... whose likeness is displayed on it?" "Caesar's of course" ...."Then give to Caesar what is Caesar's and give to God what is God's".

Jesus is so smart. He saw that trap coming from a mile away. I would like to have that kind of wisdom in my interactions with people.

I do not want to waste my time rolling joints of my above averageness just so I can get a momentary buzz. I want to use whatever God has given me to get to know him. If I want to get to know someone, the easiest and most natural way to develop friendships is through pursuing a common interest.

When we walk along side someone, with our eyes focused on a common pursuit, a job, watching kids, taking a class etc, it gives time for the friendship to grow. A three hour deep conversation at a coffee shop right after you meet someone would be too much. We often need time and a common pursuit.

God is a person who has interests. If we want to know him, we can start by doing what he is doing. If we are not spending all of our energy displaying our brains/body/bank we are free to do what God says which is "understand and know me, I am the Lord exercising loving-kindness, judgment and righteousness in the earth. For in these I delight." Says the Lord (Book of Jeremiah 9:23-24).

God enjoys showing kindness to people...do you? Are you becoming the kind of person who manages his own kingdom well enough to help others manage theirs?

God enjoys truth. He can judge in way we cannot, but are you the kind of person who is increasingly learning how to speak the truth in love to the people around you? The words you say do stick with people. There are times when you may have something true to tell someone, but you may decide to hold off. This is one way of speaking in love. It may be that the person will not be able to hear your truth about being content as a single when you (the speaker) are happily married. Or, the person may be able to hear truth from you ,but he is not in a peaceful enough frame of mind to receive what you are saying. It would not be loving to tell him then, just to relieve you of the burden.

God enjoys making things right. Do you enjoy being known for not participating in office gossip or for regularly giving (time/money/energy) for the benefit of someone else's kingdom without expectation of return?

Your brains/body/bank allotments are all like monopoly money. It's yours for awhile and you may be known as the one with a hotel on Boardwalk for an hour or two, but before you know it all the money goes back in the box, your horse or shoe is piled in with the houses and hotels, the board folded over and the box is shoved under the bed.

God and his kingdom last forever. Monopoly is a fun diversion, it's not real life. Real life is about getting to know God and learning how to use every ounce of brains/body/bank he has given you for HIS glory and for the benefit of those around you. Even if you are the most beautiful person in the world, you may only see yourself in the mirror 15 minutes a day. The rest of the world gets to see you for hours and hours. Who you are is not to be used for your addiction…it was given to you by God and he wants to train you how to manage who you are and the kingdom you have for an eternal purpose.

Summary:

God gives people a wide variation of brains/body/bank. It may not seem fair to us, but he must be happy with the arrangement. Human beings are susceptible to seeking glory, praise or respect from other human beings based on their comparative allotment. God gave us our brains/body/ bank so others would look at us and give glory to HIM, not to us. We are to go after knowing God more and using all we have been given to point to him.

Discussion questions:

Can you think of any other ways people take hits of glory for something God has given them?

Why is it soooo tempting to seek praise and respect from other humans?

How does the story about the mark on the wall help you gain a perspective on God as described in the Old Testament?

Can you talk about one story from Jesus' life that makes him stand out as someone you would want to get to know?

9
I am in this for the Fellowship

I started this book by telling you about my fence poles. A few weeks after I got all the fence poles in the ground, I was ready to put up the wire fence. Kirsten tried to help me, but it was too heavy. Some friends said I needed a come-along and a tractor to do the job right, but I had neither. I shared my dilemma with my friend Sean and he said he was the solution. You see Sean got the large version of the Irish genes and he was confident in his ability to be the human come along. On the next Saturday, he came over.

He had only two hours so we got started right away. We rolled one of the four sides out and nailed the fence to the poles. It was going faster than I had expected. We rolled the wire around the corner and I realized I had a problem; the corner pole was bending in under the strain of the wire. This would not work. I needed to put wooden braces on each side of each corner pole. That would take time and Sean would have to leave soon. I was frustrated.

I grabbed my chainsaw and ran off into the woods looking for a little tree to do the job. I cut up some poles and was walking/running out of the woods when Sean passed me going into the woods. I shouted some directions about where to find the next pole and kept moving. He stopped and shouted back, "Hey, I am in this for the fellowship." The what? I thought...I am in this for the fence.

I like Sean and all, we are still friends, but I was thinking only about the task at hand. I had always wanted a farm and with Sean's help I was going to have one before lunch.

Just like it never occurred to me that Sean was helping me that day just to be with me, I never thought of Jesus and the great commission as his opportunity to be WITH us. Once I took seriously my decision to follow Jesus, I had more of a "the house is on fire, grab your bucket and get working, no time for talking" approach. Life was a sprint to run the race for God and dying on the track got you extra points.

When Jesus said "make disciples of all nations" that to me was the "there's the fire, here's your bucket, we'll talk when the fire's out" directive. It never occurred to me that Jesus could have stayed alive for enough years to visit every known people group and village in the world himself to get the job done. After all, if you want a job done right, better do it yourself. Getting the word out about faith in Jesus and teaching people how to become like him is the primary job at hand, but Jesus wants more from us than just a "get 'er done" mentality.

Paul tells us God enjoys working through us and in us at the same time. Once I understood what Jesus had done for me on the cross and what it meant to put my faith in him, I felt I knew most of what I needed to know. Sure I wanted to learn more of the Bible and learn how not to sin so much, but first and foremost I was ready to get on with the job.

Jesus said that every student who is fully trained will be like his master. At first I was interested in having the power that Jesus showed on the earth. Wouldn't it be nice to have the power to do miracles, heal the sick, cast out demons, and raise people from the dead? Is that what I can look forward to if I progress in my God knowledge? Maybe, but I won't get there by focusing on the power. More than acquiring power, I want to become a Jesus like person. What can I do to be active in that endeavor? I know God alone can make me a better person. I know I can resist those changes by sticking with my habits and attitudes. But how can I participate?

A key change in my life came when I began to focus not only on what Jesus said, but on what he did during his earthly life time. For example, Jesus fasted. Until this time in my life, I saw no reason why I should fast. Then I started thinking, if it was good for Jesus to do, it might be good for me to do, after all, I want to become like him. Why not at least try to do some of the things he did and see what happens. So I started by fasting for 24 hours one day each week. I did this weekly for about five years and now I do it when I am teaching or perhaps travelling or going into an important meeting.

I learned several things. The first was that I tend to treat people based on how I am feeling. If I don't feel well, I can be grumpy. When I am hungry, I don't feel well. But I had to learn on these weekly fasts that I could not be a jerk to my family for a whole day once a week for years to come. I had to learn to focus on something other than my desire to eat to make it through the day. This helps me to seek first the kingdom of God when things are not going my way in my own kingdom. I recognize that my irritability with the slow service does not need to be evident in the way I speak with the store employee. Our bedroom is in the middle of a remodeling project right now. I don't have a place to put my stuff and I am annoyed. In my kingdom, I always have a room with a place to sit down and store my stuff where children don't make forts and my wife does not redecorate. A martyr's death by fire seems more manageable at times than certain living situations. However, I do not have to speak to the rest of the family angrily just because I do not have a place to put my stuff. Instead I can tell them I am annoyed and irritated about the situation and ask them to pray for a godly attitude while I am restoring this small part of my kingdom.

Fasting also taught me how little power I really have. I can't go for long without having to stop and refuel. I can't be that important in God's great scheme of things if he made me so limited. Fasting has taught me to face my limitations more readily and recognize that unless God is working through me at the time, my efforts are pointless, no matter how holy the task appears. Fasting has also taught me that the real power to live comes from a connection with him not proximity to food and other physical enjoyments. No matter how good the pizza is tonight, I will still be hungry tomorrow. A life spent pursuing food and fun alone is a life wasted.

During those same five years, I also spent 3 hours each Thursday afternoon alone with God in room at a local retreat center. Sometimes I read scripture for a long time, sometimes I wrote in my prayer journal, but mostly I sat and did nothing. It was hard in the beginning. The silence was ringing in my ears and sometimes I had to get up and walk around. Sometimes, I fell asleep for awhile. I never heard an audible voice, but I know God used those times to quiet my soul and teach me to listen to him. Doing nothing during prime hours of the day was tough. It did not feel very productive. Like a good American, I like to be productive so I can enjoy dinner and an evening of relaxation. Now I see how God was teaching me to wait on him. Without those years, I doubt I would be able to do the work I am doing now.

We are about to enter our 6th summer of our ministry in Mexico. As many as 50 people a week stay with us at our Irish monastic center called Cuirim (Keer-um) House in the slums of Nogales, Mexico. We spend our days in rhythms of prayer, study and service to the poor in our community. This year many of our groups have cancelled because of the news reports about drug cartel activity and the swine flu epidemic. We have not had any outbreaks of the flu or gang activity in our area, but people simply are not coming this year.

Instead of ramping up for the summer right now (May), we will have to be content waiting for next year. A less mature me would have been scrambling right now for something significant to do. A more Jesus trained me knows there is something else he wants me to do. One of them was to sit by the James River as I am doing right now and write this book. I have been talking about it for years, but have never had enough mental space to sit down and do it.

There are other activities known as disciplines which Jesus can use to form you: scripture memory, service, joining a small group.........Engaging in these activities does not commit God to doing anything. One student told me, doing these activities (fasting for example) is like holding your cup out in the rain. You can't make it rain, but holding your cup out will help you to catch whatever God chooses to send you.

This same student came up to me one day and said, "Brian I finally get why it is so important to become like Jesus right now instead of waiting until we die. At the beginning of the lines for the roller coasters there is usually a yogi bear telling you how tall you have to be before you can ride the ride. That Yogi bear is like being a certain stature in Christ-likeness. If you are too small in Jesus, the roller coaster of life will be a scary ride, instead of the joyful experience God intended when he came up with the idea. And the safety bar represents the commands of Jesus (Don't worry for example). Well if you are too small in Jesus, those commands are a double whammy. Instead of keeping you in place for the ride, you are so small that they keep smacking you in the face on the way down. It is bad enough be scared the whole way, it worse go through it getting smacked in the face with 'Thou shall not worry' too."

We can't make God come be with us, but we can bar the door when he gets there. The thoughts we think, the words we say, the choices we make, these can all be like debris thrown in the doorway, blocking his way. He stands at the door and knocks…what will you do? Most likely your opportunity will not be heralded by an angel, but by a phone call or a child's request for Cheerios. Quick prayers for God's perspective have saved many a day from ruin.

Summary:

Jesus did not put us here just to do work he did not want to do anymore. He created the work opportunity so could be together with him as we work. As we work alongside of Jesus, we can make efforts to become like him by living life the way he did. For example, choosing to fast for 24 hours is doing something Jesus did. God is not obligated to bless us or be impressed just because we fast. It is just basic wisdom to emulate the practices of a person we admire.

Discussion questions:

Can you give an example of someone who is more like Jesus now than they were in the past?

How can holding on to habits or attitudes get in the way of becoming like Jesus?

Can you describe a time when you got stuck in a negative attitude and missed some moment in life? Or can you describe a time when you got stuck in an attitude for a long season of life?

How can you relate to the description of life as a rollercoaster?

10
Whatever it is

Jesus did not show up and say…"suck it up…just a few more years and this will all be over." He said, "I have come to give you abundant life…I have come that your joy may be full. I give you a peace that passes understanding…go make disciples of all nations."

Which motto would sum up my life? Do I walk through my days just trying to get through or do I look like someone who actually likes his life. I have my discouraging days, migraine days and sad days like everyone else, but taken as a whole what is my life about?

When I was eight I had a favorite ride at the amusement park. There were these little cars and a kid my age could drive, really drive. You turned the wheel and the car moved. After a few trips around the tracks, I made a sad discovery, if you let go of the wheel, the car went around the track anyway. There were two rails under the car and they kept the car from going off track, not me.

The Ten Commandments are like those tracks. The first few cover our relationship with God and the rest guide our relationships with other people. Even if a culture were to ignore the first few but kept the rest, the citizens would get along relatively peacefully. Think how different our culture would be if there never had been any murder, lying, stealing or adultery in real life, or in the media.

I used to think God was like lifeguard at our neighborhood pool. A quarter of our pool was set aside as an adult section. A thousand kids could be bobbing up and down like fish in a barrel and one elderly woman could have a quarter of the pool to herself. Any kid who dared duck under the floating plastic divider would hear the lifeguard's whistle blow followed by a command to come sit by the wall.

I saw the pool as the range of possible human behavior and sin as an arbitrarily roped off area like the adult swim section. Everyone knew the water was the same on each side of the divider, but the owner of the pool decided a certain area was off limits. I could understand roping off an area with murder and maybe lying in it, but a lot of the other stuff labeled "sin" I thought should have been left as part of the big pool.

Now I know that if God says it is sin, it is like putting orange juice in your gas tank. If he says don't judge lest you be judged...I don't want to judge. If he says don't worry...I want to stop worrying. I believe him even if I do not understand him. But I need help.

Paul says we are supposed to take every thought into captivity to the obedience of Christ. I need Jesus to help me learn to manage my thoughts. My thoughts about something or someone often precede my actions and statements. If I can learn how to bring every thought captive and obedient to Christ while it is brand new in my mind, I am well on my way to living the abundant life.

I know enough to be aware that it is often not the event at hand (car breakdown, change of plans) that is the problem. My response is the problem. The lingering effects are not usually the event itself but how I reacted to it, the decisions I made, and the way I treated people in the process that make for the crooked poles in my life.

I was a volunteer in a youth ministry years ago and in that group was a very quiet young man. We tried in vain to get him to talk, but he hardly ever said a word. One day we were sitting around talking about our favorite vacation activities when he surprisingly spoke up. He said he loved to go to his cousin's house somewhere in Florida or Georgia and wait until mid-night. Then he would sneak out and go into the swamps, walking in until the water was up to his chest. Lowering his head to the waterline he would scan back and forth in front of him with a flash light until he saw to eyes looking back at him. Then, he would jump and grab it... "Grab what?" someone said.... "Whatever it is."

I must constantly scan my mind to bring my thoughts into the light, kind of a Jesus microscope, to see if they should be allowed to keep swimming around. If it doesn't look right, toss it out. Little alligators are better tossed out right away. I change channels quickly and skip parts of movies because I do not want new little alligators. I leave conversation circles as quickly as possible when talk turns to gossip, fear, judgment or other junk. I simply don't want those thoughts swimming in my mind.

You may have thoughts about other people when you see them. Don't ponder them, grab them by the tail and toss them. You may be plagued with little negative alligator thoughts about yourself…phrases like, "I'll never amount to much, I am always such a loser or my family would be better off without me". Grab 'em and toss 'em.

Jesus brought us good news. God's kingdom is not way off on Mount Olympus, it is right here in our midst. He taught his followers to pray "thy kingdom come, thy will be done here on earth as it is in heaven." You can invite God into your little kingdom to teach you how to manage it his way. That is what it means to be a disciple, a student.

When I read the gospels, I marvel at how well Jesus lived in every situation and I want to be like him. I know one day that I will stand before him. I am right to fear his judgment for the mistakes I have made, the times when I was focused on the wrong thing. But I also trust there are times when I have pleased him and I want the next years to more of the latter.

The grace of God is a wonderful thing, it is new every morning. Looking back I have some crooked fence poles, but looking forward I still have some ground before me. What will I do today, this week, this year to make a straight line to reigning with him?

My first steps in becoming like Jesus included the weekly activities like fasting and three hours of solitude shared with you. I still practice those but not rigidly. I may enter another season of weekly disciplines in the future but this season is different. My current season of life has no pattern right now so I have learned how to embrace life situations as growth opportunities. During the first summer at our center in Mexico, we faced several kingdom challenges.

In my ideal kingdom, I get 7 hours of uninterrupted sleep, a prerequisite for being a nice person the next day. Sleeping well was not a guarantee of a kinder me, but a sleepless night got the grumpy me 10 times out of 10. Our son Levi was 1 ½ that summer and he woke up almost every hour on the hour the whole summer.

My wife and I were so tired we could fall asleep waiting at the traffic light. We did not need to fast from food at all that summer to learn how to lean on God, we were fasting from sleep.

At our center we often have 50 people living in a very small space with our room right in the middle. We have 4 kids and all six of us stay in the 12 by 14 foot room. I am an introvert and I greatly crave my time alone. I need it as much as I need sleep. I am such an introvert that I have a headache when I leave church from talking with everyone and I need to go home and take a nap just to get out of the fog. At our center in Mexico, we chose to put ourselves in a place where there was no place to get away, knowing we would have to depend on God in new ways.

These experiences have freed us from expending so much energy trying to get things just so in our kingdoms. Having small children is a wonderful way to learn from Jesus how to seek first his kingdom. With children you constantly have to say, "Not my will but yours be done". I have thought of creating a toddler belt designed to carry multiple Sippy cups and a day's supply of gold fish just so I could focus on something for more than 15 minutes.

Jesus knew what he was talking about when he said anyone who gives a cup of water to one of these little ones shall by no means lose his reward. I have given out 100,000 drinks so far so I should be set. I honor God when I see these requests as opportunities to grow and love, rather than as interruptions to my kingdom pursuits.

For many of us, keeping our own little boat afloat consumes us. God does most of his molding in our own little worlds, but he wants us to step out. He wants us to use what he has given us to bless those beyond our little circle. Over the past 5 years, our family has been working in one little neighborhood in Mexico. In the grand scheme of things it may not look like much, but because God has blessed our efforts. As I sit and write this book in Virginia, 2,000 miles away in Mexico there are 100 children eating at the little kid's café we set up three years ago. Our family wants to seek first the Kingdom of God and his righteousness, so do the many people who help serve and supply this little soup kitchen. It is not right that children are hungry. Today a group of us have merged our kingdom resources to make it right. Satisfied children are swinging on swings and going down a slide right now because a church in Maine chose to give the kids a play set. It is a beautiful thing.

The very act of giving away from our own kingdoms changes us, frees us, and gives us life. God did not design us to be containers...we go bad if our kingdoms fill up and stagnate like little barrels on the shipping dock.

My hope in sharing all these stories is that you will see your life in Christ as an every moment thing. I hope you find great joy and purpose in encouraging those around you to learn from Jesus how to really live. I am still teaching my children the basics: close the door, don't spill, eat in the kitchen and God is still teaching me the basics: love the Lord your God, speak the truth in love, consider others before yourself, and seek first the kingdom of God. Hopefully I will be a quick learner.

Discussion questions:

How has the book helped you have a different perspective on your own life?

After reading this book, what are a few things you could say about the Kingdom of God?

How does viewing your life as an opportunity to reign with Jesus help you through the ups and downs?

30160795R10039

Made in the USA
Middletown, DE
15 March 2016